IS THERE LIFE AFTER THIRTY?

Are you~~ ~~
turning~~ ~~

drying with disgust

curling up in sadness

peeling from their branches

paddling in the winds

drifting toward the cold ground

but it's the first day of May?

If so, this book is about you. It is an invitation to revisit your disgust and to revive your hopes. You will view the "little deaths"—the ones you feel now. And you will discover hints about "living hopes"—that sense of fresh life you need now.

IS THERE LIFE AFTER 30? is about young eyes looking with shock at a stubborn world refusing to touch her problems. It's about novel ideas bouncing on the cracks and holes of old cement. It's about new hearts feeling pain with every man living like crumbs under the table. It's about eager spirits running around in a locked room. It's about curious hunters chasing shadows in hope of light. It's about spring flowers thirsting for an early morning rain. *It's about being young, but tired.* It's about the Resurrection and hopes turning green.

IS
THERE
LIFE
AFTER
THIRTY?

PETER L. STEINKE

AUGSBURG PUBLISHING HOUSE
Minneapolis, Minnesota

IS THERE LIFE AFTER THIRTY?

Library of Congress Catalog Card No. 77-135229
International Standard Book No. 0-8066-9441-6

Manufactured in the United States of America

for my parents,
who are living hopes

IT'S A MATTER OF TASTE

Disgust tastes bitter. Your lips sting. Your tongue is scorched. Your nose wrinkles. Your hand rubs your mouth.

You take a drink. You gargle. You spit. You don't feel like eating. Or trying. Or living. You shout.

Take a look beneath your griping, because you are groping. You are not life's latest party-pooper. You're its newest pioneer. You are looking for light, an open door, hope, a new day, possibilities.

Listen above the noise of your own shouting. Hear the sounds of hope: "Behold, I make all things new" . . . "Behold, I have set before you an open door, which no one is able to shut . . . "

Explore! Underneath and above. To the left or the right. Over here—maybe there. In "Negatives" search in your own neighborhood. Young people share with you their bitter taste of today, the world, adults, themselves. "Tension" is a probing ground: where disgust and hope clash, where yes and no shout at one another, where death and life shape your loyalties. "Possibilities" are hints about Resurrection life styles, about life and death matters—but life matters most.

Wrestle with life as it is! Reach out for what it can become! Squeeze your questions! Dig your feelings deeply! Touch the sores of man! Come, dance with God's promises! Choose your possibilities. Taste the hope of new life. Today is always the first day, a new day, a green dawn, a day for resurrections.

CONTENTS

JOE AND ME

It's kind of scary lying here, thinking. Being alone. Poking into myself. Wondering what's going on outside these walls. Depressing. But I like the privacy. Just being alone. Getting away from everything that bugs me. No pressures. No deadlines. No arguments and stuff. None of that crazy screaming—"Hurry up! You're always late." . . . "Will you please turn down that jungle music?" . . . "What are you up to now?" . . . "You can't do anything right!" How I like to be at a distance from all that. To be separate. Only me. I guess it's just a feeling that there's a me. I feel safe here. I'm private property. No trespassing. No one owns me now. I can play my music. Think my thoughts. My room. My pictures.

Pictures? There's the one Dad can't stand. My boy, Joe Namath. Dad says Joe has a bad mouth. "But he believes in himself," I keep telling him. "Big deal! Take it down! He's a jerk!" Dad thunders. I guess parents can't stand someone who believes in himself. Parents or no parents, Joe stays. This is my room, my own world.

Anyway, I like a person who stands up for himself. Is that a crime? It's a lot better, at least, than being a wet noodle, flopping all over the place. Letting people wrap you around their thoughts. Knotting you up in their rules. Who wants to be curved into somebody else's wishes? You could never become sure of yourself, of what you do and say.

Well, I wish I had more faith in myself. Some guys are really cool. They know what they want; they reach and stretch for it. Success! They get it. So they try again. But how do they do it? I want in on the secret. There are things I want and strain to get. Plop! Down I go. Once I fall short, I feel stupid. Then I promise myself never to do it again. Inside there is a vote of no confidence.

And my parents are no big help. They run me down. Starting out in first gear, they say, "Why don't you participate in more things? You're not going to amount to much hanging around here. First we wasted our money giving you piano lessons. You never practice anymore. Then we had to push you to play Little League baseball. Now all you do is fool around with cars and read magazines." Soon they shift into second gear: "Why don't you make something of yourself like others your age? At this rate you'll end up as a ditch digger." Finally they're in third gear, roaring down my neck, "You're a disgrace. You should be ashamed of yourself." It's maddening.

When I try to explain that I don't care to do what they want me to do, they're backing into reverse. The speech begins again. What's the use of saying anything, they don't listen. Crazy! I know—just know my mother listens to herself not to me. I keep telling her that I can't do what others can do. They've got it—interest and ability or whatever—I don't. So what does she say? "Don't compare yourself with others. Comparisons are foolish." Well, what in the world has she been doing for the last fifteen minutes? Comparing me! Comparing what others do and I don't.

"Comparisons are foolish." Huh! Hardly a day passes when she and dad are not comparing—not just with me. What someone else did wrong. How so-and-so thinks wrong. How do they know somebody else's thoughts are wrong, anyway? Because they are adults. Oops, there I go. Dad says I'm too cynical. Didn't even know what the word meant. So I used a dictionary — "snarling, distrustful, gloomy." Maybe? That still doesn't give them the right to compare people, to push them under the rug with one sweeping sentence.

Why is so-and-so the way he is? Find out about him before you cross out his life. Perhaps he's had a ragged life. The world whips him with ugly words maybe. Just like my parents do. Anyway, they never walked over the same ground he did. It's dumb to knife people. Most of them are bleeding already. This cutting up and down stuff—Lucy rips into Charlie Brown . . . Chop . . . cut . . . chop . . . clobber . . . chop. What's left? Pieces.

Good grief, everyone seems to think he's right. Can't hack that. "I'm right, you're wrong. I know, you don't. Listen to me, not to him." Big men talking little things. They have bad mouths. If you can't believe in yourself, I guess you have to tear down others. "They are all alike—no good." . . . "I helped myself. Why can't they?" Sure, Sure. Comparisons—me against them. Disgusting. Why can't it be you and me . . . us? No. It's me against them.

Fill in the blanks. Please print. Name . . . address . . . telephone number . . . age . . . male or female . . . height . . . weight. The blanks are filled. But it's—it's those other blanks. Why aren't the important questions asked. What would you like to do? What's your experience? How do you feel about it? Where are you going? How would you explain it? Blanks . . . solid blanks. You write down vital statistics but not your real feelings. Oh, I wish people could share *themselves,* not just stiff facts. Why are people afraid of feelings? Are they afraid of themselves?

Okay, everyone is for or against many things. Just respect what the other guy feels. Differences don't have to divide people. My dad likes to tell me, "I know what you are against, but what are you for?" He says I'm against war, rich people, school, church, adults. Well, he's against Joe Namath, higher taxes, the Supreme Court. What's he for? Why can he be against stuff but I get chewed out for it? I just can not think and feel exactly like him. He can't think and feel as I do. You can't argue feelings.

But he has to have the last word. "In my day kids knew their place. In my day they respected authority." He's always giving me a history course. . . . Crummy history. It's my day now. His days are gone. How can I relive his day. "The Lone Ranger rides again. Hi-ho, Silver." Oh, sick. It's now . . . different. How can he say he understands me just because he was a teenager once? A teenager, yes, but only once upon a time. Not today. Guess I'm being cynical. The lone cynic rides again. Hi-ho, Aluminum.

He's not too bad, though, Could be worse. Works hard. He's not going to tear up the world—just Joe Namath. I just can't dig him sometimes. Can't figure out why he doesn't want me to go through what he went through. Then he turns around and says what was good for him when he was my age is good for me now. Mixes me up.

Kind of creepy, Joe, digging inside and floating outside of yourself. I hate being alone when I feel this way. I know! Think about God. Cheer up. Chase away your doubts. Dump your lousy feelings. Beat your chest and say three times, "God." Here's the prescription—add two tablespoons of sugar to your sauerkraut. Shake well. Garnish with spice and all things nice.

What do you have? Terrible, terrible tasting sauerkraut. Man, when you're feeling low, you can't simply think God. You've got to feel him.

Cynic. That's me. The whole world is one blob of cynics. Dad's super-tongue shoots: "You're going to set the world aright. You and your soul brothers have all the answers. That's a big laugh." and Mom adds, "Dear, you're only 16." I don't mind the 16 —but that *only*. How would they like it if I kept telling them how *old* they were?

Well, Joe baby, I better get up. Off to the cage. Thrilling. Two plus two equals four. A halfback dash to get a seat at the cafeteria. Surprise quiz in the afternoon. Big surprise! We get them every day. Then, get this, Joe, a talk with my counselor about my future. I'll tell him I'm going to straighten out this world. That's what I'll tell him. And he'll say, "Yes, yes, I see." You know what that means, Joe? You are only 16. Too many cynics in the world, Joe. What do you say?

For the man who hates the thought of being average

I'M THE HOLE THAT I'VE DUG

ME:

"Blasted room. Too damp in here. I hate being in this hole. Out. I want out."

MY ROOM:

"Wait a minute. Have you forgotten? I am the hole you dug. I'm yours. No one else lives here. At any time you can come here . . . sigh and relax and escape. But why do you sit here pretending to dislike me? Your abuse is, after all, ungrateful behavior.

ME:

I crawl into you, I admit. There is no force or coercion. But blast it! You're always here. Your arms never refuse me. Your eyes cover me. Personally you bore me to death, that un-changing stare. It's as if . . . **ah, like** . . . you own me.

MY ROOM:

Okay, I stare. But it's to welcome you. When no one cares, you can come here. It's private. Moreover, I don't insist that you change. More than satisfied . . . yes, I am . . . to have you stay just as you are . . . and, well, to keep our friendship like it always has been. Tell me—do I question your actions or reject your love? Now, you know I don't. Come in here and you have no need to wander off foolishly into unmapped territories. With me you are safe. Untouched. Unjudged. Besides, I let you control me . . . whatever you want, I let you do. So what if I stare at you? Is that so hard to take? At least, here you can catch your breath, untighten your anger. No one can come here but you. Ha! I don't like the parallel, but I'm like a locked bathroom. I'm all yours whenever you wish.

ME:

Yes, you're right. However, was it a mistake to dig you in the first place? Too easy . . . it's too easy just to return here. You're no challenge. You never offer resistance. I keep coming back . . . too easy to crawl into . . .

MY ROOM:

Hold on! What's wrong with that? I keep your secrets. I'm loyal to you beyond a shadow of a doubt. Who can compare with me? In here you don't have to fight off fears, cover up your tears. All can be said; no one will ever hear. I'm easy, yes. But I'm yours, and you are free.

ME:

Free? I'm beginning to doubt that. I come whenever I wish. I do whatever I want here. But free? Really? But *why* do I come to you? To be free from that which I can't control. No doubt about that. But I'm afraid to be for something; to take the knocks, to take a stand, to take a chance. Is the price I'm paying worth it? You see . . . I . . .

MY ROOM:

You have chosen me to safeguard, protect you. I'm your freedom. Try to fill me in—cover me up—don't come here. But you can't leave me altogether. I won't be tricked. You need me too much.

ME:

Yes, but that's the problem. I depend on you to think I'm free. But am I?

MY ROOM:

You're only as free as you think you are. But what kind of freedom would you have without me? People could crush you, tell your secrets. Here you are private, your own master.

ME:

You know, I like it here. But the problem, the whole rotten trouble, is I'm private. There are no people.

Can I be free only when I'm in my hole, when I'm the master?

MY ROOM:

Suddenly you have a strange fascination with freedom. I don't know what it's all about. When you're here, you're always free.

ME:

Oh, that's why I can't stand your stare. It covers me. It's just like when I'm outside of you. I'm covered. All around there is this large, covering, all-seeing and knowing eye. Whether I'm inside of you or outside—I'm always in a hole.

looking for

Behind every "I do"
lurks a
"Can I?"

WHERE DO YOU FIT INCH?

Have you stood on a high place? Looking below is like viewing through a microscope; everything is small. You think that you could reach down and put the cars in the palm of your hand. The trees could be snapped, you think, as easily as a dandelion.

But you feel small, too, as space expands for miles and miles. Now the world looks like a blown-up balloon. That's hard for me to accept, being small myself. You feel like a one behind a decimal point and a string of zeros. You think, I'm just an inch in a world of miles.

Nowadays people don't think in inches, do they? The sign reads: Kansas City — 150 miles, Historical Marker—1,000 feet ahead, 20 yard line, 50 yard line. To feet and yards, especially miles, go the headlines. So you become 1/12 or 1/36 or 1/43,360 of most everything. You're lumped in a line of inches. On both sides of you another inch is rubbing shoulders with you. You're lost in the crowd, the dozen, the numbers.

Your cousins don't have it much better. The ounce gives way to pounds and bushels, quarts and gallons. What a nuisance a penny is. It takes up more room than it's worth. So what happens? Like anything else, if you're not worth much, you're placed in an institution. For the penny, useless and bothersome, that means the piggy bank.

Where can an inch be just an inch nowadays? Only in rows of inches to make a foot? Or a yard? How can an inch think much of himself if he always thrown in line with inches? I have to be an inch, just me, before I can become the fifth inch or the hundredth or thousand and fourth inch. After all, you couldn't have a foot or a yard if it weren't for each inch.

When will people learn to care inch by inch?

$.59 LB.

I work in a supermarket—produce department. It's not the best-paying job in the world, but it gives me scratch money. In fact, the money is okay. The customers bother me, though. How would you like to be a target for complaints all day? "The peaches are too hard." "Your bananas are overripe." Sometimes a comedian makes the scene: "Hey, young man, your lettuce looks like it has been sleeping in its clothes for a week." Or, "They sure don't make oranges the way they used to." Funny, huh?

The worst ones are the money groaners. "Tomatoes? Fifty-nine cents a pound? They don't look very good. Too soft. Your price is too high." Poor tomatoes! I don't know how they can take it. Picked up, tossed down and in between slandered. Some ladies pinch and squeeze the tomatoes. Others whirl the tomatoes around and around, looking for spots and redness, I guess. By the time we sell them, the tomatoes ache all over and feel dizzy. There's one nut who spins the tomatoes in the air and catches them. Who knows what he's doing? Maybe he's testing their velocity or gravity or something, or just likes to exercise our tomatoes.

And the ears of corn? What they don't do to them! Right in front of the other ears, some lady is busy undressing an ear of corn. You'd be surprised how suspicious people are of corn. A customer said, "Don't you have any corn without worms hiding inside?" I looked at the ear she disrobed. Nowhere could I find a worm or even a brown spot and told her so. What did she say? "Can't you see the prints of their footsteps?" Could you believe it?

Getting a rough deal is some of the apples. Big juicy ones with perfect shapes sell first. But the small or crooked ones hang around for days. Usually they don't sell until we put them on special.

You know, it's funny. Customers look for the right color, the right look, the right feel, the right shape with analytical precision. But if you put something on sale—tomatoes for instance—color, look, feel and shape don't seem to matter much. Now customers have the right price. If you can get it cheap, get it. Sell it below the original value and there is little fuss.

I wonder if our customers treat people the same way.

GOOFED UP GOOFING OFFS

SOUR . . . sour is what I feel when I can't get what I want . . . or don't know what I want. Sour is an emotion . . . stinging, scratching, biting. When everybody else wants what I want, I feel sour. If nothing works—you know, you push button after button but no lights go on—it's not worth the effort . . . that's feeling sour . . . Question marks twisting your feelings . . . isn't anything for real? . . . that's sour.

GOOFY . . . goofy is a feeling too . . . it's lightness, a moon walk, people and music, not just people . . . always people *and* music. I feel goofy when my questions go to sleep . . . it's like floating, flying a kite. To goof is to feel alive . . . goofing off the tension, the thumb-sucking, nail-biting, and heart-aching. The opposite feeling of goofing off is goofing up, and that's kind of sour. Goofing up is bloopering, messing up, being tight . . . when you're really goofing off, though, goofups aren't too bad . . . like making a mistake, but laughing. When you're goofing off, all goofups are jokes you play on yourself.

SOUR . . . it's a feeling that eats away at you . . . like your goofups. Sour is letting your goofups take over . . . you can't get *off* your failure.

GOOFY . . . but that's like being a ball taking crazy bounces, or singing nonsense songs in the shower . . . sort of punchy. Goofy is . . . well . . . just doing something for no reason at all, not knowing if you're on the left side or right side . . . even if you did, you don't care much.

SOUR . . . is feeling goofed up.

GOOFY . . . kind of like feeling . . . ah, if you're a breeze . . . charging into a sail gently but firmly. Fun . . . real fun to make a sail boat dream down the lake . . . or tickling the leaves on the trees . . . or playing checkers with pieces of paper on the ground.

SOUR . . . that's me . . . goofed up and can't goof off. Why do I believe so seriously, so devoutly in my goof-ups? I worship my failures. Then . . . like a jerk I make fun of people instead of making people fun . . . a jerk's a poor joke.

GOOFY . . . that's what I want to be . . . off not up . . . off to have fun for fun . . . and others. You know, to be good for laughs. To become a child . . . who laughs naturally . . . who is like a breeze . . . goofing off.

It's the truth
the whole truth
and nothing
but the truth...

NO ONE
HEARS
FEELINGS
(Letters to a Listener)

Dear Pastor:

In case you haven't guessed, Pastor, this poem is written in moments of timid, if not defeated, hopes. It is not meant to condemn or accuse, but merely to demonstrate the too-average feelings I have towards existence. I bet you think I'm a case! However, you are the person who encouraged me to squeeze out my feelings. Like you said—if you cheat on your own feelings, you become afraid of them. And your feelings are you. Why live in fear of yourself? Won't you soon hate yourself as well? So here goes. Maybe you can share your feelings about the poem (and me). Remember: No cheating!

Luke 2:40

"And the child grew and became strong, filled with wisdom;
and the favor of God was upon him."

Grow.

Come out of the safe cocoon of childhood.
Leave behind the wonder warmth of youth.
Science and the calendar and convention
all say it is time
to put away the moonbeam dreams
to forget the fairy stories.

Go

Make a place for yourself in the world,
bend and adapt

change colors
shape yourself to fit
train yourself to accept the packaged sympathy
                              the prefabricated care
                              the polyester smiles.

Learn to move as part of a whole

for if you dare to move separately you will
no longer belong.

Time has had enough of those who lead.

Follow as a shadow and a whisper.
   Once you knew the sky
   (but the real sky is for children)
   Once you reached to touch rain
   Once you loved
   (but love is for the ageless and you must
   age).

Grow.

Abandon your curiosity
Leave your laughter lovely
and you will soon be an adult.
            (so why are you afraid?)

Looking for the way,

The Kid

Dear Pastor:

Thanks for saying hello last Sunday—no one else did. My major peeve is the coldness in church. What happens to the warmth of God's love? Isn't it supposed to thaw out man's ice-cubed heart? I can't stand a 30 degree Fahrenheit worship service. If the church dies, as someone predicted in today's newspaper, I believe the autopsy report will read: the Body of Christ froze to death.

So I wrote "Psalm on Parchment." It's my view of cold, habitual church attendance and frozen worship schedules. Don't suppose you could use it for the Old Testament lesson next week, do you?

Psalm on Parchment

And the people go to church
   each man woman child worshipping his own
   private God
mouths forming words to hymns
tongues moving in memorized kyries and
te deums and agnus deis
   gospel lessons
   epistle lessons
   old testament lessons
   brushing like futile moths on the polished pews.

After church the golden cross

   will sleep amid yellow pages of a closed Bible
   wrapped in plastic swaddling clothes
   or die within a wax lily.

There are no more meek shepherds,
   the bearded prophets are laughing,

the gilded gates
   the forty days and forty nights
   the pillar of fire
     all are gone.

The cup of oil lies shattered on the parched ground
of the Promised Land.

And the people go home
   shaking hands with the preacher
   smiling compliments for his excellent unheard sermon.
Then the flowers are taken away
the hymnals rearranged in their racks
the floor swept.
   Finally the last custodian leaves
   locking the great door behind him.
         And who would care if God
         should rap angrily against the lid of his
         stained-glass coffin.

I really should write more happy poems. Grief and disgust, however, are so much easier to convey than joy. I write what I deeply feel, and often my happiness is too shallow to be expressed well. Besides, if I feel good, I'd rather talk than write. So, if I do create poems on lighter themes, they're mostly about things immediately around me— the seasons, colors, feelings of the air, a flower I like. If you're wondering why I criticize religion so stringently, yet write nothing in praise of it, it's because I have not yet developed my talents (?) enough to tell how I feel about God personally.

Looking for the Warmth,

The Kid

Dear Pastor:

Things are getting worse for me. Inside of me feelings of disgust over-populate themselves. What am I disgusted with? Here's a listing from page one (Volume 1) of my anguish:

> push-button love
> amateur human beings
> cellophane words
> thin vision
> dyed truth
> stale enthusiasm
> iron institutions
> shatterproof ears
> automatic handshakes
> one teaspoonful of dreams

I can already guess what you will say to me: "Hypocrisy has nothing to do with chronology." You know my nausea with systems, rules, adults, the way things are. Likewise, you know my distaste awakes my anger from its sleep. So you'll say phoniness is within and not with age. Sounds great, Pastor. But I'm still mad. For so long older people have told me: "That's reality. You have to be realistic." Okay, it's reality, but it's also evil. Do you want me to embrace it or pass it off and live with it?

When will someone get up and shout, "I have a dream." But we crucify or shoot dreamers, don't we? Shouldn't our beliefs make dreams? Isn't that realistic? I mean for a Christian's life?

I feel confused. I need a voice.

ADULTIE

What's it all about, Adultie?
Is it just for the past we live?
What's it all about
when you think it out, Adultie?
Are we meant to change here and now?

And if only authority counts, Adultie,
then I guess it is wise to grab power,
and if life belongs
only to the strong
what will you build, another Babel Tower?

And as sure as I know
there's an earth below, Adultie,
I know there's something that can grow
something even non-youth
can know.

I know about hope, Adultie.
Without eager hope, we just exist, Adultie.
Until you find hope
you've missed, you're nothing, Adultie.

When you run, let your dreams lead the way,
and you'll find hope any day, Adultie.

Waiting for a Voice in the Wilderness,

The Kid

Dear Pastor:

You haven't seen me around church lately. After bouncing back from my latest attack of disgust, I've had a relapse. What's bugging me? Well, if you'll recall, about six weeks ago you picked some horrible hymns to sing: "Onward, Christian Soldiers" was one. That was followed by "Stand Up! Stand Up for Jesus / Ye Soldiers of the Cross." Then the troops stood up for the pre-battle pep rally and sang "Fight the Good Fight / With All Thy Might." Do you think the congregation is filled with God's Green Berets? All I see there is a pack of scouts and brownies trying to win merit badges and growing goose pimples with talk about being prepared. Did they go out to fight for Christ with faith? Did they go "onward" and "stand up" in the face of injustice and persecution? No, they didn't! Not one member of our

church signed the petition Jill passed out on decent housing. So here
is my psalm by the suburban shepherd:

The System is my big brother,
I shall not want;
it makes me lie down in gray indifference.
It controls me besides the busy computer,
it manipulates my soul.
It leads me in streets of law and order
for its name's sake.

Even though I walk through the concrete jungles of death,
I fear no violence;

for the System is with me,
its guns and its legislation
they comfort me.

It prepares housing
in the presence of mine enemies.

it anoints my neighborhood with favoritism,
my property is protected.

Surely security and mediocrity shall follow me
all the days of my life;
and I shall dwell in the restricted homesites
of the System forever.

Looking for the Home of the Brave,

The Kid

Dear Pastor:

Thanks for your visit last week. I didn't expect you to get so angry. You really exploded. But it didn't matter. You listened to me. When you do that, you can get mad as you want. You heard my feelings; I got your message, too.

However, I'm not ready to come back to church yet. My feelings need rearranging. Neither you nor my parents have answered my question: do you or don't you destroy a man's faith if you put it in an institution? Somehow you have to move a man's faith to do more than usher or attend meetings or work the bake sale. If God is the *author* of faith, why do you put him in a *footnote?*

No poems this week . . . no more questions. My feelings have run out of ink. I need a refill.

God must have ears for feelings.

Waiting for the Wind to Blow,

The Kid

A BREAK FOR excitement

NO WRINKLES

Around our house it's fish on Friday, chicken on Sunday, and leftovers on Monday. Every week! There's no change in the menu. My grandmother did it, so my mother has to do it. I've suggested changing the order, if not the dishes. No luck. Not even minor alterations.

Get this—my mother bakes egg shells in the oven. Then she crushes them and spreads the pulverized shells around the bushes outside. Her mother used to do that, too.

What's wrong with changing? Man, I can't take it any longer. I'm not going to let my life become a merry-go-round of etceteras. We live like wheels going in repeated circles. But why can't we live like a triangle or an octagon or rippling curves for once? But that's the way everything seems to be now: do it the same way—in circles.

Don't you think we live in a perma-prest society? No ironing needed . . . no wrinkles or creases or changes. Keep everything in line. Don't ruffle the feathers of routine. Make life stable, calm, familiar with the old way, the set way, the only way you've ever done it. Sure, life is neatly pressed, intact and established. But if you want to live like a triangle, why do the circles insist on making you live like circles?

People laughed at the Wright Brothers and Fulton and Ford. Edison was a fool; Burbank was some kind of nut. Jesus, too. They weren't etceteras; they were exceptional. The ordinary became the miraculous.

Some things cannot be packaged and salted. For instance, you'll have a stiff-necked attitude toward people if you freeze your feelings. Pickle love and it will turn sour. Put peace in moth balls and you clothe your wars in noble slogans. Make everything circular and you miss the wisdom of half moons, the fun of triangles, and the surprises of sharp curves.

Keep life the way it is—like yesterday. But what about tomorrow? More fish, chicken, and leftovers? I'd like a hamburger, please!

MAYBE/ UNLESS

My English teacher asked the class to write a composition on responsibility. I tried. But after a couple hours of thinking, scratching out words, doodling a little, flipping over some records, and a stiff headache, I gave up the obvious failure. To get my mind off the comp tragedy, I looked at my magazines. In one of them I saw this picture of a baby. Then I thought: things seem just to happen for a child; he is free, plays around with everything. When a child messes around, he is making all kinds of choices. He responds all the time with ease.

So I had a brilliant idea. In my comp I wouldn't use capital letters or commas or periods or complete sentences —no floors, no ceilings, doors, or windows to hem in the words. I'd let the words go free . . . fall like the pieces of a puzzle . . . not fenced off or walled in . . . sort of like the words were playing on the paper. To be responsible, I thought, there has to be freedom . . . where words can mess around . . . not bound by grammatical rules. Grammar is obligation, but responsibility is doing something you want to do. You can't chain responsibility between a capital letter and a period.

As you can see, I'm back to "good grammar." My teacher missed my point. She wrote all over my paper. However, I still believe responsibility is freedom, playfulness, wanting to do something. Read my paper. What do you think?

maybe . . .

  someday

    his ad libbing

      his unrehearsed smiles

      his in-to-everything fingers

      his sponging ears

      his quick fascination with
        bright red

      his exploration through

        chewing grass

        paper

        biting legs of

        people

        chairs

his prowling to know

    where the candy hides

    how red orange blue talk

    which sounds tickle or scratch

why the moon doesn't fall out of
  the sky

to create

  triangles out of squares

  hats of newspapers

  hugs of kisses

  friends out of sharing toys

will   slowly   be

  bent like a pipe

  regulated like a clock

  vacuumed like a rug

tall people with

  big hands

  loud voices

say and say and say
  and say and say
  and say and say and

  draw within the lines of the
    coloring book

  raise your hand

do not touch what does not belong
    to you

look at the picture and see what
    I see

follow the words of the story with
    your finger

stop talking during rest period

soon he will be

    stuffed in a room

      glued to a desk

        spotted for chewing gum

          steeped in Dewey
            Decimals

given a book . . .
told to close the book . . .
given a book . . .
told to close the book . . .

    repeat

    facts

    as given

    in order

    in the blanks provided

    (and put your name in the
    right-hand corner of your paper)

and he will be

    class-sectioned

    IBM-ed

    red-penciled

    report carded

    filed on record

    (and wood carved for
      School Board XYZ)

but

mistakes will dent his grades

    chill the patience of others
      with him

    nag his parents

    brand him

his self-confidence
      d
        r
          o
            p
              s

he thinks
    if—then
        if—then
            if—then
                if—then

if he is successful
    is well behaved
    can prove himself
    can memorize
then he is
       valuable
       worthable
       acceptable
so he will be ashamed
  of his mistakes
    suspicious of himself
    feeling weak in the shadow of
      another's strength
    unloved with conditions
      attached
feeling like a door
    pulled from the outside
    pushed from the inside
Yes
  the problem is
    he will live—
      much
      below
      the
      line

      of
      his
      possibilities
as
    a similar facsimile
    a carbon copy
      a ditto-ized clod
      a xerox duplication
    a parrot
    an echo
    a masquerade
the problem is
    he will not be
    helped to live
      as himself
      with trust
      in freedom
         to mess around
         to wonder
         to laugh
         to ad lib
         to live
            in response
unless . . .

ANSWERx
ANSWERx
ANSWER=
ANSWER³

When you're young, you need answers with teeth and claws. Why do some adults think you need every answer they can give? A few sharp answers can carry you along better than hundreds of answers smooth as sand.

I need answers that hear fresh, smell honest, and grip my mind. It could be one word. Maybe the answer I need could be simply two open ears and two understanding eyes. No, too many adults feel compelled to give me answer times answer times answer.

I won't buy canned answers. That's why I like the answers I find in some songs, movies, and bull sessions. They're like picking fresh flowers. Adults give me answers packed in cans with the same old labels on them. They don't think the issues over for themselves again or let me look at the situations from different angles.

Don't you gag over the stuff they tell you? For instance,

"We've had the problem for over one hundred years. No one is going to change it overnight."

No kidding!

"People will be people, you know." Now there's a swift insight. One plus one equals two.

"You have it good. Don't complain."

Isn't that the usual putdown?

"I can remember being like you at your age, rebelling. Take it from my experience. You have to learn the hard way."

Well, thanks for the encouragement. I can't take it from your experience —I've never *lived* it.

Left or right. Up or down. In and out.

There's an answer, and another answer bumper-to-bumper with the first. Pull out the old Latin maxims, the proverbs granddad used, rhymes. Or begin with, "They say . . . " Or, "As everyone knows . . . "

Well, you can keep your platitudes in the file cabinet. I don't need answer times answer times answer. The length and width is unimportant— the depth counts. Give me an answer that cuts deep—with claws and teeth.

When you pile on the answers, you're telling me that you want to give me *advice*. But your advice seems to be given for your own peace of mind, not my needs. Do you know why I want answers? For encouragement. . . .

NO, INC.

"Wipe your mouth with a napkin."

"Tuck your shirt in."

"Sit up straight."

"Stop talking like that."

"Where did you go?"

"Why were you so late?"

"How many times have I told you?"

"Grow up."

"Be careful."

"Take your time."

"No!"

"Don't!"

"That's what you think."

"Who are you kidding?"

"No!"

"No!"

"No!"

"You're so careless."

"Make yourself useful."

"How can you be so helpless?"

"What? Do you think
  I'm made of money?"

"Why can't you act normal?"

"No!"

"Don't!"

"You should study."

"You should mind your
  own business."

"You should stay home
  once in a while."

"No!"

"You never ask."

"You always leave your
  clothes on your bed."

"You must have your
  own way."

"Stop it."

"Cut it out."

"Knock it off!"

"No!"

"Don't scratch your pimples."

"Don't pick your nose."

"Don't bite your fingernails."

"For the last time—NO!"

They hammer in the morning, and they hammer in the evening. With shouting gavels they pound out their sentences: "No, don't, should, stop." You become dizzy, and mad. You can't stand trial every day. When I was four or five, I could take it better. Now I can't stand it. If they would just tell me once in a while *why not*, I wouldn't half mind all the no's and don't's. Ask why not, however, and you're suspected and accused of another crime—rudeness or lack of respect. My criminal record is getting so long soon I won't care what I do.

When you have the power to say no, you can idle someone's enthusiasm. But I refuse to be tugged and shoved with words and no reason. Besides, I'm a person, not a problem.

THE JOLLY GREEN GIANTS

Why aren't Americans foaming with happiness? No one comes close to our gross national product. Some time ago I heard lopsided figures that we have 48% of the world's wealth but only 7% of the population. But why doesn't the bluebird of happiness build her nest in our land? We're a bunch of grump bugs. Right now, I bet, some group is percolating a pot of complaints for more pay or about the high cost of living.

If we have nearly half the world's wealth, what's it like to be part of the 90% of the population who must share the other half? Except for the rich guys, millions of people must have sad faces stained with tears. How unhappy they must feel.

Money can't buy happiness, they say. But "they" don't act like it. Take my father, for example. From the time he was 16 until now at 53 he punched in and out five times a week. He's accumulated everything he could. So I asked him: "Why did you do it, Dad? How did it make you happy?" He raised his voice, saying, "Why did I do it? For this house. For you. So you and your sister can get an education. That's why!" I answered, "No, I mean did your getting ahead help other people get on their feet? What did you get out of it? A sense of satisfaction, joy, purpose?" Of course, I was very popular around the house after that. "You're ungrateful. I'll teach you." My allowance was stopped. My car privilege stripped; my dates limited; my hours restricted; my presence ignored. The only thing added and not subtracted was time for homework. Strange, don't you think, how more algebra, biology, and history was the best answer he could offer to my question.

He's real touchy about the subject. But I wanted to know how making money and accumulating things gave a sense of purpose. I still want to know what money does to you. Are people really the only things money can buy?

Sometimes I feel that's true. I get the idea that I'm a product my parents have produced for profit. My father says he has "invested" in me . . . that he wants me to be a "credit" to the family . . . that I'm family "stock" . . . well, I'm not his profit—or his debt.

Oh well, money can't buy happiness. And I'm not for sale.

VIRTUES IN SHEEP'S CLOTHING

Why all the purple fuss about lost virtues? You can call ambition, thrift, and moderation virtues if you want. I can't. Man doesn't do *anything* unless he can get something out of it. Ambition is a generous term for selfishness. Thrift is an excuse for stinginess. Moderation—well, that means play it safe.

Somewhere—can't remember where —I read about "virtue is enlightened self-interest." In other words, act like a smooth operator, a regular Joe, a nice guy, dripping with smiles and flashing sincerity. Above all, sound as if you're the champion of apple pie and brotherhood. Simply add saccharin to your well-chosen, compromising words. But don't get caught. Avoid any transparent statements . . . just generalize with ideas. As far as I'm concerned, virtue is being a smart phony. It's playing the game of get what you can but don't get caught.

There are fabulous rewards . . . it's worth the chance. Awaiting the virtuous man are gold watches, brass plaques, silver rings, red carpets . . . and a coppertone tan. That's virtue: stay on top of things, play the game to win.

Lost virtues? All we've done is taken off the sheep's clothing. Underneath the garb there is a wolf . . . sly, sneaky, crude.

Moderation is an excuse for being a coward. Thrift is a sleek word for greed. Ambition means taking advantage of opportunities and people —and the goodies in the process. Virtues? Or vicious vices in gentle grammar?

Virtue is to be a man. What kind of a man? To help another man become a man . . . not dependent on me . . . but a man in his own right, with his own worthiness to stand on. In place of moderation and thrift and ambition, I place real virtues: a man who is a living, breathing first aid kit, a man who can weep with another, not just compete with him, a man who can be turned inside out, a man who isn't thin-skinned or sheep-skinned, using pretty words to skin alive another man for petty goals. "Beware of false prophets!" said Virtue Himself. And he was a MAN.

THE SLAYBOY PHILOSOPHY

We, the undersigned students, have prepared a statement of grievance. Having been disturbed by recent events, we felt compelled by conscience and concern to express what we deeply feel and honestly think.

The grievance is not an enumerated listing of specific wrongs or injustices; neither is it a demand for meeting our particular wants. Too many grievances are merely emotional reactions to current crises, which touch upon symptomatic or surface manifestations of the problem. It is our contention, whether the conflicts are of racial, political, or generational nature, that the *causes* of these dilemmas must be considered, discussed, and attacked. Repeatedly, the problems confronting our world, nation, or local community are handled with mercurochrome, gauze, and band aids. Seldom is surgical incision, cutting into the root of the illness, suggested or practiced. Moreover, there are some irrational and insensitive groups of people who contribute rash, angry, and demonic solutions to our problems, cursing the facts, the presence of disruption and destruction. For instance, if the foot hurts or kicks, cut it off. In both cases, however, a band aid or scissor approach, the nature of the crisis is untouched or disregarded.

Our grievance is not with any specific group or general range of principles. It's a grievance with an *attitude*. In our opinion attitudes determine actions. What all of us are witnessing in these confusing days is not only oppression and repression, revolution and riots, but also an attitude toward life. It is an attitude of fear, resentment, and suspicion.

Furthermore, the attitude is informed by a subtle yet prevalent philosophy. We have chosen to call it the "Slayboy Philosophy." This view of things has been drummed into us through every structure of Western life. At the center of the "Slayboy Philosophy" is a simple tenet: be one up.

To be one up, each of us must gather weaponry. Some have accumulated status symbols of wealth and position as "weapons" against social rejection and economic weakness. Rigid principles and right doctrines are used as "weapons" against those who would think imaginatively. Deodorants, hair tonic, and dress fashions, though seemingly articles of offense, have become actually "weapons" to capture the feminine prey. Even tests, again, whether for a driver's license or civil service job or physics, have been transformed into "weapons" to hold back the advance of possible enemies. Sex, an automobile, a title, and so on, have been used as part of the militia in being one up. War stands out as the exemplary notion of one-upness on a grand scale.

Why have we never been asked to question the assumption that one-upness is necessarily, naturally, or primarily the best way to live? Our grievance is in the form of a question: why haven't we been taught to be *one with?* If competition is necessary for free enterprise, but it excludes the conditions and motivations for community, we believe the freedom is illusory, mere sloganeering. Freedom without interrelatedness is not freedom. It is an excuse for self-interest.

What we see in conflicts around us makes us aware that there are many *ones* who are *down* and more who are *zeros*. The one-ups, who keep the other ones down or make some people nothings, have learned to employ everything as potential weapons to "slay" those who wish or pursue to be ones. Consequently, the "Slayboy Philosophy" fills out the attitudes that shape the actions, which are disturbing to each and all of us.

Our grievance is a human one. Why must our humanity be justified or proven by how high "up" we are in relation to others? The only genuine humans we know are those who are one with others and thereby are not justified, but completed.

Roy Langley

Ivey Sands

Dick Comolli

Jackie Christiansen

Jean Kristopp

Woody Houston

god who?

LIFE IS ONLY A RUMOR

"And God saw everything he had made, and behold, it was very good." To you it might sound strange, but for me "everything . . . very good" means—Mosquitoes didn't bite. Poison ivy didn't itch. There were no stubbed toes or splinters in your finger. You couldn't find a crooked nose or an ugly face. At least you never noticed. There were no people,[1] people,[2] people[3]—just people.

People weren't in a hurry. No one minded stopping for a red light. When the light changed, you didn't hear the burp of a horn or the sizzle of tires. In fact, no one even knew what a siren sounded like.

And speeches never sounded dull. Flooding the air were sounds of the cat dancing with the mouse, the rain chanting with the wind. You could hear the apples whistling at the grapes bursting out on the vine.

Can you imagine having leaves for a wardrobe and liking it? Too good to be true, but girls never worried about their weight. You could wash and set your hair as little or as often as you wished, but it never really mattered.

In the beginning you made life. It was a poem you wrote, a pie you baked, a hand you held, a flower you planted. Your laughter kissed someone's heart. You could feel the color of joy, see a smile sing.

And, of course, there was plenty of chatter.

It was "very good" to be alive.

Now I wonder, though, if the world is going out of business. Man's obese pride, his two-ton load of self-interest, bruises the flower of human dignity, bends the stem of the spirit, jars loose the roots of peace.

And above the landscape diesel fumes and sulphur gases and hydrogen pillows attack and devour the sky.

And within the neighborhood—hate's uncomfortable humidity swells the differences between men and dampens community spirit.

And we live like rush hour traffic: hurrying to school, hurrying to the hairdresser, hurrying to meetings, hurrying to picnics. We may be lost, but we're surely making record time.

But we can't hear the hunger turning into anger. We hardly notice the dented hearts rustling, peeling, crumbling. Black becomes blacker. Red becomes redder. White, whiter. Strangers grow stranger. Time grows shorter. The road narrows. Death laughs longer.

What's the choice? Fake it and make it? Go along and get along? Or else? The truth: who tells? The gimmick: it sells. Can more of everything make everything "very good"? Or, have numbers only swelled expressways, beaches, nerves, prices, cities?

Please cancel my subscription—life is only a rumor.

eath in the disguise of dis-
s the most and best of you,
le of life tapers. Thin hopes.
openings. Shy courage. You
le into boredom, which is
lling life short. Ho-humming
y through life, you are dull
smooth. You have no sharp
view; you feel powerless;
you don't count; you col-
ur confidence; you judge
you're nobody; you don't
yourself; you don't believe
f anything. What's possible?
Not even a hearty, defiant
nly a limp, "Oh, well."

an turn to self-pity. Poor
cked on! You become as
ith others as you are with
r self-pity licks its wounds
g, damning others. Then
ing on your complaints
ration and overstatement.

Everything is the *worst*; nothing ever
works; you *always* lose. What's possible? Very little! The "Aagh!" inside
—too hot to handle—boils over into
"Damn it all!"

Or, you can frantically clutch everything. "Now or never. At once. Presto. Right now!" It's all or nothing.
You are ready to destroy anything—
your own dreams, your own courage,
your own judgment, your own neighbor. To smash all doors at any costs
is the mad reaction of believing in
death. Disgust is a tantrum death
throws into your life—a wild fever of
grabbing, demanding, seizing. What's
possible? Nothing! A violent "Aagh!"
—"The hell with everything."

Giving up, tantrums, curses, kicking,
inflated accusations—then the haunting hush. And a strange whisper after
the whirlwind, "Why not?"

DEAD ENDS

When you are young, you want life
to taste new, to move suddenly, to
make sense, to groove. But it doesn't.
It zigs and zags, jutting to the left
and skidding to the right and bouncing flat. You call "heads" yet it always seems to end up "tails." You ask
for a light, but get a burnt match.
What is said and what is done come
out in different shapes. Some say to
you, "Cheer up!" but you know that
if they ever smiled, their faces might
crack. Inside you feel like jumping,
but you sit still in your fear. You put
on a happy face; still, it can't cover
up your downbeat moods. Zig and
zag and zoom.

When you are young, you yearn for
fittings (ties that match your socks)
. . . meetings (sockets that fit your
light bulbs) . . . balance (answers to
even your questions) . . . exchanges
(lips pressed on lips) . . . companions (like thirst and coke). But life
tips, ricochets, and vibrates. Little is
smooth, even. You feel at odds.
When you're polka-dot, others are
plaid. Become a plaid and the world
becomes stripes.

The contradictions, the differences,
the ambiguities, the disagreements,
the paradoxes, the discrepancies—

squeeze and twist and bend the eager beat of life.

Life is "Aagh!" It's nausea. "Aagh!" —a ripping sigh from tightly stretched feelings; a gasp leaking out of punctured hearts; a grunt of a beaten spirit; the hiss of hope running out of steam; a steady dripping of enthusiasm from a broken faucet. It's choking on melancholy.

It's "Aagh!" with parents. "Aagh!" for the heavy rules. "Aagh!" for the nagging "you should do this and you should do that." More "Aaghs!" for boring talk, hounding shouts, and crabby faces. It's "Aagh!" among the zig zags. No zip or zap.

Perhaps the sharpest "Aagh!" you stick into yourself. What you are and what you want to become feel miles apart. You wonder: Am I a "lemon," a misfit, a verse out of rhyme? Am I a switch that is off more than on? A ten chapter book with only one chapter? A movie with sound but no picture? You wonder, as knotty disgust tightens you inside: Who put the glue in my freedom? Is there a lot to live? After the dry days and dead ends?

It's like you're walking along a path. But suddenly walls stand before and around you. You change directions. Left. Then right. Zig. Zag. You stop. But you want to go. You hear voices saying to you—

"You can't move the walls. Can you climb it? Too high, huh? Well, stay put. You're going to look for a door? Okay, but. What? Did you find a door? Good. It's locked. You don't have a key. Wait your chance.

"Now where are you going? To see if there's another door. You won't listen. There is! What? It doesn't have a knob on it. Try prying it open with a knife. Hmm, that won't do it. Push your weight against it. Harder. Again. It still won't open. Use your knife again. No? It won't budge. Are you sure? Okay, okay, you're positive. Take a break. Give it a good kick!

"Where are you running? I can't hear you. Oh, you see another door. Why are you stopping? Someone slammed the door in your face. Oh, no! Scream! Holler! Shout! Tell him to open it. Why doesn't he open the door? He keeps saying that he doesn't want any. I bet he thinks you're a salesman. Tell him you're not. He refuses to open the door . . .

still saying he doesn't want any. Reason with him. Tell him you have an I.D. card and good references. No luck? Forget it. Curse him! Throw paint on the door. That'll show the fool.

"It's hopeless. What did you say? One more try. Okay. It's your life. What sign? There's a sign. What does it say? Exit. Don't go through it. You have to find an entrance door. I can't hear you. You're shouting too loud. You're making me mad.

"What are you doing now? You're going too far away. How will you find the path again? Why don't you listen to me? Stop shouting at me! What do you mean, you never asked for my opinion? It's your own fault. Don't blame me."

Dead ends. An exit instead of an entrance. No key, no knobs. Closed doors, slammed doors. "Stay put." "Curse—Kick." "Take a break." "Don't blame me."

Disgust. "Aagh!"

What's the use? So what? Who cares? Forget it!

But why? Can't polka dots go with plaids? Are doors only to be kicked?

BEGINNINGS

Hope begins in its own absence. With trouble. Against a wall. Outside doors. Under darkness. With tears, nerves, and headaches. F's, minuses and flat tires. "Don't" or "I can't" or "I won't." The beginning of hope is at the dead ends, the closed doors—and a whispered question, "why not?" Then a glance. A turn. A step. A knock. Maybe two or three steps. Another knock. "Yes, why not?" A fresh breeze. A flash of light. A sudden sound. Unexpected —"Aha!"

Hope is the "Aha!" forged out of "Aagh!" It's a light cracking the darkness, angry shouting humbled into an easy chant. The zig becomes a zip; zag a zap. "Why not?" Space expands; color brightens; cold melts; joy dances, fresh air lightens the breathing.

Hope is the invitation to begin again, to leave the hiding places, the stopping places, the nowhere places. It's a stubborn yes in spite of over-populated zeros; it's the dawn freeing itself from the night; it's spring lying in wait through winter for its sudden explosion—covering the earth with its perfumes and dazzling the skies with a fashion show of color. Hope is life's way of wiping away tears, tossing aside fears, and getting ready for a birthday party.

Life begins in birth. It can continue only by believing in new beginnings, new births. A whisper—strange, sudden—"why not?" It's life struggling to be itself. Hope is the way life begins again; it's a reminder to dying vitality: "Be yourself." Life and death matters, but life matters most. That's hope.

Hope is the refusal to let life die. Out of death comes life. After the funeral comes the birthday. The locked doors are all entrances. At the dead ends there are new beginnings. "Why not?" The whisper becomes a shout—"Happy Birthday!" And hope answers "Aha!" It's life regaining its bounce. Joy is the pleasant surprise of hope. "Ha-Ha!"

But hope doesn't grow on trees. No vending machines carry it. "Don't worry" or "Cheer up" or "Things will get better" cannot shape hope. There are no push buttons, or formulas, or proof for hoping. What guarantees are there that hope will work? How do you know what doors can be opened? But that's the point: hope begins when everything seems hopeless. There's no guarantee, no favorable statistics, and no demand. Only promise.

So hope waits, not with its fingers crossed or tapping its toes. Hope waits like you wait for a letter. Hope is like a halfback who won't go down —stretching, straining, twisting to get free. After being *downed,* hope tries again for the first down, a new beginning.

Out of loss and failure, at the closed doors and wits' end, hope begins to take shape. Precisely there life struggles against death. And life can only be itself when it becomes free of death. But disgust is fearing death. Disgust is a judgment on yourself. It's choosing exile, captivity. It says more about you than the world. But hope is believing you can come home again, feeling free to live with that promise. Can anything *begin* without a promise?

God has a bag full of surprises. You can't outguess him. He's always pulling off the unexpected. He's more difficult to figure out than a hundred algebra problems. He won't act on demand or for rewards, but he's up to something. He is not a computer you can program. He will catch you by surprise.

But why surprise? That's simple. God acts only by promise. How, when, where the promise will be kept comes as a surprise. Out of the blue. He cannot be controlled. Anyway, if you could control him, how could you trust him?

Your muddy feelings, tied-up thoughts, and tissue paper hopes are real—you want to give up, maybe run away. But, once again, this says more about you than God's promises. You feel worthless, unloved. So you conclude you have nothing to give. Perhaps you hate yourself. And you passionately hate those who make you feel more worthless. Then promises seem fragile. You want better guarantees. However, it's only when the guarantees, and the demands, fall short that the promise can surprise you. Granted, promises don't look too good from that angle. But look at the promises from this angle: all the promises of God find their Yes in Jesus Christ. Now there was a surprise. Out of death came life. If you can trust God's Yes, in the middle of your own No, you will be surprised. Throw the bag of his promises marked "yes" at his feet, and do not give up until he pulls out a surprise from his bag. Jesus Christ is God's Yes to life and no to death. He is your hope that there is a resurrection at the dead ends. When there is hope in resurrection now, the big surprise is that you try again, you begin.

DREAMS AND DEMONS

You find yourself throwing in the towel. One game is lost, but you feel the season is ended. Deep inside you there is a feeling of wanting to try again, but you keep saying no. Nothing defeats courage like "No!" And if others, especially people who are important and near you, say "No!", hope loses its color quickly.

Much of your disgust is with what is real: polluted answers, wilted smiles, sawed-off truth. You don't like what you see or feel or hear. The clouds and the nightmares are too obvious. Where are the rainbows and the dreams?

Well, that's where you come in. You can choose to give up in disgust or to give way to your dreams. Disgust is a demon, a power that would strangle and control life—closing doors, narrowing space, shortening breath, casting shadows of fear, paralyzing the moment, shutting out the vision, chaining to the failure of the past. To dream, however, is a power to flirt with possibilities and to start from scratch. Dreaming is hope taking shape: putting purple buttons on a red shirt, knocking on doors when it looks like no one is at home, asking a new question when everyone else is contented with the book's answer.

Dreams and demons . . . it's a struggle between life and death. You bounce back and forth with feelings of being out of it or with it. You scratch your fears, yet itch with anticipation. There are moments when you're at odds—only to turn around feeling even.

Life is both onions and roses. Seldom is it ever one or the other. At times life is like a traffic jam with monotonous stop-and-go conformity. But it can be like breezing down an open road. Life can be demonic, a captivity to harsh forces . . . like a fly caught between a closed window and screen, mapping a zig-zag pattern with furious buzzing. Or it may be like a bee feasting buffet style in the garden. Life is *both* dreams *and* demons. It comes in liquid and powder, color and black and white. The important point is what you choose to let it become. Do you fertilize the disgust or hope? What shapes your life? You can stay flat on the back of disgust or run the risk of hope. Can you climb over your limitations? Or do your limitations climb on top of you? What's your question: So what? or

What's up? In a sense, people never die; their dreams just fade away. For what you dream of becomes what you finally live. Are you held in check by the demons or free for beginning again? What shapes your style of life—dead ends or beginnings?

A Christian style of life includes both the dumps and the clouds, both the onions and roses. There is disgust and hope. The life style of the Christian is death and resurrection, dying and rising. It's feeling the sharpness of slaps and bruises and the light-heartedness of handshakes and hugs. It knows the cut of failure and the healing of forgiveness.

What happens in Baptism—dying and rising—is the style, shape, of life in Christ. Jesus himself told his disciples that he must die *in order to* be raised. The promise of God, his Yes in Christ, surprises you. Hope out of disgust. Beginnings at the dead ends. New life out of old failures.

Without death to what you do not want to give up, there is no life. Oddly enough, you do not want to give up your disgust very easily, either with yourself or others. You find it hard to handle your failures, your negatives, your hatred. If you experience death disguised in disgust, you may begin to believe that's the way it is. Final death terrorizes you since you experience it so heavily right now. You cannot accept God's Yes to you. When you die by confessing your own dead ends, you will find God can handle it. More than that, God can surprise you with new hopes. The past is forgiven; the future is open; the present is possible. Resurrection!

Death and resurrection. Disgust and hope. Demons and dreams. There is no need to deny death, to cover up disgust, or to hide from the demons. They have limited rights. Why act as if they have more power than they do? Life matters most. Resurrection is unlimited. You may refuse its power or deny its hopes. But nothing you feel or do can undo the fact. The Resurrection of Jesus Christ makes all things new and possible and spacious and now—even when there is little proof or hope, when everything seems old and limited and narrow and hopeless. After all,

disgust is your judgment on yourself; hope is God's gift for you.

Is there life?—the nagging question of disgust—is the beginning of hope. For you wonder, if there is little life now, what about later? If systems, circumstances, and adults persist in saying, "No!" and you reply, "Aagh!", what life is there after 30? Or if the world trots madly on its course of business as usual, what about the life of the unusual—the poor, oppressed, the nobodies? If you're tired, weary of hoping, and dreams are empty . . . the bitterness rages. It's a time to die. That's your choice.

God's decided, though, to make any time a time to begin. It's only a promise. But where else can you begin?

Is there life now, after 30? A man who was at the dead ends, knocked around by closed doors, drooped in a crouch with doubts, said: "Where there is forgiveness of sins, there is life and salvation." God can handle your negatives and hand out hope. Death and resurrection. What shapes your life—your own "No!" or his "Yes"?

To live in the style of Christ is to die and rise. You die to the limitations you place on yourself. God can make you come alive with possibilities. You die to the captivity of your disgust. He can make you free to live with hope. You die to your past failure. He can make you start afresh.

Here are five possibilities for living in the style of Christ, in death and resurrection. They are not exclusive. For each style overlaps the others. But basic to all is the understanding that life is both/and . . . both deaths and resurrections. Moreover, the little deaths of now are necessary for resurrections, new beginnings.

Is there life after you become 30? After you are conditioned or comforted? If you feel others are "dead" after they become 30, it is because they chose to die and refused to believe in the promise of possibilities, in resurrection. It must be remembered that your present disgust, a disguise of death, is always and ultimately your own choice.

If there is no resurrection, the promises of God are vain and your hopes are dead. How can you begin again if there is no promise? Or possibilities?

Hope is not a promise things will get better, or be more to your liking. It's the risk of acting—in the hope that something new can happen and promises can be trusted.

ADVENTURERS

It's dark. Your eyes pace back and forth like a radar screen. You look for a crack in the darkness, a point of recognition. As you sniff suspiciously for peculiar sounds, your eyes shift. A blurred sound draws your ears to attention. Momentarily your eyes freeze on the spot. There's a slight movement of your hands. You clear your throat hoping for a response from the darkness. No sound. Very little movement. But you stand there with all your senses turned on, ready for something.

Under the ceiling of darkness, you probe with your eyes, hands, voice, feet, and ears. In the light you fall in line—sort of take things for granted. In the darkness, however, you carve and slice your way, adventuring with new sensitivity to movement, sounds, shape and sights. You can see more in the darkness than in the light. In the darkness you probe. Little is taken for granted. There are no maps or statistics to check. No pat answers. Perhaps you trip over your own two feet. Or you brush against a tree and step in mud. You may rub your hand on a wall, searching for a switch. In the darkness you venture with your whole being; you turn the dial of awareness to the high position.

The Adventurer probes, gropes, questions. He enters strange neighborhoods, not knowing his way around town. Here he does not know the druggist by name or what dogs bark but don't bite. For the Adventurer hope is a passport to unknown and untravelled areas. The secret of the Adventurer is that hope is not shut down by closed doors or strange sights but by satisfaction, the silence of non-care. There's darkness, but risk, venturing. And risk is the infallible sign of hope.

In adventure, taking risks, putting workclothes on courage—the darkness is the beginning of life. You may risk and fail. But he who takes risks and fails can be forgiven. Out of the darkness can come the light. But now the light looks different—you're aware of life around you, grateful for it, because you've searched in its absence.

The adventurer is one who chooses not to die now, darkness and all regardless. Rocking chairs and familiar doors are left behind. The Adventurer believes in resurrection, new light, open doors, making friends out of strangers. For he believes the Resurrection is God's big, big surprise. It's a new light on your darkness, but only if you have probed the dark, searching. God is unpredictable. His bag is not full of facts and principles; God's bag is full of promises. In your darkness he throws his light . . . as he promised. So you take risks in the dark. Your hope is venture into birth. You'll be surprised!

HOPEES

You are in a slump. Over and again people have said, "Keep plugging away." And you do. But your plug doesn't seem to fit in many places. Failure produces pressure. You feel like "No. 2" and try harder. Now you feel like "No. 3" and not trying at all. It's a lonely feeling. The old chants: "Give it another try" . . . "Go ahead" . . . "You can do it if you want to" become hard words. Resentment bends your ear when such phrases are spoken. You want to but can't. So you try only what you feel you can do. And that may not be much. You know it. Besides, you do not believe you are valuable, but small and puny. Anyone who might reinforce this feeling is hated—including yourself. When you want to but believe you can't, you feel like an island, a desert . . . cut off, and a small slice of life at that. A drop in a bucket. It's not so much that you're at dead ends as a feeling that you've never even started. You have not given hope a slight fling, a first chance. You are not fed up with life, rather, very hungry for it.

Maybe—only maybe—that's where hope can begin. Fresh energy is untapped. Your own resources lie untouched. Disappointment has not yet cemented into bitterness. You're heading that way, though. In all likelihood you are still teased by the question, "Why not?", with the possibility that maybe—only maybe—you really can plug in somewhere, somehow, someday. Each new "plug in," no matter how small or unnoticed, is enough to keep you wondering, maybe I can do more than I believe. At this time you are merely wondering, not believing. But you can't shake off the possibility that what you want to do may be what you can do. You sit on the fence. Just maybe.

The resurrection of Jesus Christ says God believes in you. Perhaps you can't believe in yourself. However, that in no way lowers or limits God's belief in you. Defeats and deaths, negatives and no, disenchantment, and disappointment can not defeat you. God has promised to bring life out of death; he is favorably disposed toward you. The Resurrection is his way of saying you are valuable. You can believe in yourself. You can't lose. When new possibilities come into sight, you can choose to go after them. Of course, you'll fall flat on your face and sprain your hopes—sometime or other. But you begin

again. Why? You believe that God believes in you. There's no instant resurrection or flip-of-the-switch-hope. You realize that falling down and starting again is a style of life.

Now there is no need to shun failure, to turn red in embarrassment and back in fear. You're not desperate like that fly caught between a closed window and screen, when there's no new birth, no sudden sound, no quick solutions . . . but just enough strength . . . to keep going . . . to believe in yourself even as he believes in you. Throw away the encyclopedia of the future; don't stuff your pocket full of answers; dare to start out on a trip with only a half tank of gas.

God believes in you. Yes, even when you feel there's not much in you to believe in, even when you just sit on the fence of possibility. Your hopes can turn green; you can try again. You can, because God can believe in you. Moreover, he can't do otherwise.

Hope begins with that hunger for life, that yes tossing around inside you but not yet bouncing and dancing. You don't need to know everything, to have the odds look favorable, to fill out an application form for hoping, to pass every exam, to pump oxygen into your dreams. You can start, begin. You can. You can. You can. God is able to do precisely that—what you think you can't. Out of death—life. Out of promise—surprise. Out of complaints—cheers. "Ha Ha!" Out of your own, "Oh, no!"—God's "Yes" in Christ. Out of "Aagh"—a sudden "Aha!"

A hopee styles his life by accepting his own "can'ts" and hoping for the possibilities God can create for him.

...you've got it made

No
matter
who
you are...

you've got it made!

AD LIBBERS

You should this.

You should that.

You should know.

You should then.

You should not.

The "you should" is spread on thick. Too thick. So thick you feel you can't.

"You should turn off the lights when you leave your room. You should follow directions. You should dress like a civilized human being. You should be ashamed of yourself."

And the "you should haves" on top of the "you shoulds": "You should have studied. You should have called me. You should have been more polite. You should have listened."

You're so "shoulded" and "should haved," you feel like an it, a thing, a punching bag for the "shoulders." Everyone wants to put you in your place. What place? Where the "shoulders" want you to be. The string of shoulds wraps so tightly around you until it feels like a heavy chain. But you resist. Why do people think they are experts about how you can best be you? They're not, you think. All they want is a you that comes close to being a xerox copy of the you they desire. You get tangled up in the you you are and the you you want to be and the you you are not and the you they say you "should" be. To try to become you is to rub against the different yous expected, demanded, and printed for you. It becomes a blistered burden . . . a feeling of being a half you, "their" you, a mass-produced-assembly-line-you . . . not your you. Your "you" can't stand on its own two feet. How *can* you be you when you are "shoulded" to be you?

You need to be free to be you. A free you cannot come about by being a drop-out-you; that is, giving up to the "shoulds." Or a free you cannot take shape by burning up all your energy in trying not to be a "shoulded" you. The you that is free cannot fold up in the shoulds. You can not be so threatened that all you can do is fight against the shoulds, having no time to become a you in spite of the shoulds.

God created you to be you. The "shoulds" can't make you you. The resistance to "shoulds" can't alone make you you. There has to be something that can help you be you . . . something that both denies the killing effect of shoulds and affirms the possibilities of being able to live out you. The Resurrection says: God can make you a new you. God has faith in his own possibilities. He is free to do his Own Thing—to make new; he isn't threatened because you feel threatened. He believes that he can help you be you. Out of the deadly feeling of *you should,* he brings a new feeling of *you can.* You can be you. You can be *free* to try again. If you should and don't, you still can. If you should have and didn't, you still can. God made you to be you. When you're not, God can make you be you . . . drop outs, cop outs, three outs are forgiven. In Christ means you are in the region of possibility. Out of shoulds — you can. Out of deadened limits—living possibilities. In Christ all things can become new. You can live to be you.

In the same breath, God says you should and you can. What you believe you can't, he believes you can. His *should* isn't an attempt to make you less than you. His *should* says you didn't, but he's still willing to believe you can. The new trick he teaches: to ad lib. You don't take a public opinion poll or check the odds in Las Vegas or scan the Nielsen ratings. You act off the cuff, on the spot. You believe that in Christ you are a new man. You can be you. At the dead end of should but can't, God can make an ad libber, a free man, out of you. Hope is saying, "I can!" And when you can't to try again freely. Don't deceive yourself—trying to be free by doing whatever you want. That leads to another kind of unfreedom. You ad lib your hope in self-giving—that's the test.

Ad libbing is the possibility of giving, because the you you want to be is the you that cares for other yous —and their possibilities. You don't *should* them. You ad lib with them. You can, and they can. And we can. Shoulders enforce conformity. Ad libbers shape a community.

"God's work must truly be our own"

GROUPERS

Hope is greener on the other side of the fence; that is, when it is green on your side. Hope is an act of people together. The mathematics of hope: 1 plus 1 equals something new . . . one plus zero equals the same old thing. Hope begins when lives touch. Draw lines, build walls, and stay alone—and you deny hope. You can never hope only for yourself. If hope ends at your doorstep, you're at a dead end. It's a selfish hope. People who need people are the hope of the world.

When you hope, you can't help but help others. You hope for new life even for the no-hopers, the hope-killers, the low-hopers. Your hope is shared not only with those who hold your hopes, but also with those who happen not to have your hope. You hope *with* pro-life people and *for* con-life people.

The proof of the hope is in the caring. Hope becomes active in love, for life is stronger than death. God gives hope to you, and you give hope in caring for those who have little or no hope.

Hope makes you a life-lover. Where death destroys life, you enter with hope. Hope flexes its muscles when "little deaths" threaten life right now. You care for people. You can't stand their hopelessness. You can give them your hope in giving your care. Hope received is hope for giving away (the only way you will keep it).

The Resurrection is God's way of acting in groups. He made life to be lived together. The little deaths of loneliness and fear divide people. But the hope of something new brings life. One plus one equals that something new. Besides, one man died so that many might live. One man was utterly forsaken and lonely so that all men might know they are loved and not alone.

Hope cares. It isn't reasonable. But it moves beyond reason. Hope cares by giving in spite of, sharing in respect of, dying in behalf of, building in place of. . . . Hope cares not because of what someone is, but in spite of what he is. Hope is present even where the results may be few, the outcome unknown, or the gesture refused.

The resurrection of Jesus Christ is God caring about life. It is possible for you to care: If you hope in God who brings life out of death, you can care in the presence of death's signs. When your hopes are green, care is green.

When hope cares, you help someone become a person. In accepting another you free him for his own possibilities, to stand up as a man. The opposite of care is control. Control is the way of death, an act of fear. You want to make someone dependent on you. In careful hope you want for another what you want for yourself . . . to be a person of possibilities, free to live, and able to give.

Hope is a group of people . . . caring for one another . . . caring when no one else cares . . . caring as if the dead ends are only beginnings for something new. It is a flow of outgoing and incoming energy. Hope is greenest in care.

FOOLS

Who wiped the smile off the face of the earth? Too many are dead serious and sad. The balloons are broken; the party hats have become helmets; instead of singing there's only blowing off of steam; where once people took turns now they take sides. Life is colored in faded yellow and status quo gray. What has happened to the laughing purple and smiling orange? In the middle of it all, the cake is untouched. The world gets an F— flunking the course in "Parties, Favors, and Joy." It's grim and grit and grumble and gooey.

The dead sure, the dead right, the dead serious, the deadbeats—frowning their eyes, biting lips, drooping ears, pulling out hair, shaking fists, expanding noses—are burnt-out hopers. No chance for smiles and funny faces to break loose. Hopes are in ashes.

Well, the circus needs clowns. And life needs Halloween and April Fools. Big hearts need parades; warm hearts —people; happy hearts—bells, trumpets, and drums. Pass out the crayons and the coloring books. Let's play peek-a-boo. Strike up the pep band. But so few will play. "That's foolish nonsense!" they say.

Life—is it a tale told by a grouch? Mother Goose, where are you? Jack and Jill won't go up the hill together. Little Boy Blue refuses to blow his horn. Humpty Dumpty sits on the wall and won't fall.

Is life a shirt-and-tie sadness? A story of dead seriousness? But isn't God telling the story? He's no grouch. In the beginning God created laughter and joy. You're skeptical, aren't you? Well, consider the giraffe—what a laugh. Or stars, the sparklers of space. A child—did his mother train him to smile? Or the sun—a candle for each new day (a birthday, perhaps?) How about the sea—a punch bowl, right? Snow—confetti? Why not?

Sounds nice, but the great party crasher, death, spoils everything—picnics, antics, comics. You know, there was a Good Friday in God's story. But — Aha! — the great story teller wanted only to thicken the plot, to build suspense. There was a surprise, a resurrection.

Resurrection—shmresurrection . . . Easter — beaster. Still skeptical, are you? So were the disciples. When they heard about it, they said, "That's silly. An idle tale of foolish women." But they often took themselves too seriously: asking Jesus to send away some noisy children, wanting seats at the head of the table, running away in the garden. Always popping up here and there, they wanted to tell the story. God won't play a joke like a resurrection on them. Grouchy guys! Dead serious followers! Looking for the predictable. Seeking success. Keeping things peaceful. But closed to surprise.

Dead serious—that happens when you think *you* are the story teller. Man is something, not everything. How tragic you are writing a silly story with dead seriousness. At the dead end of your own story, where you believe you are everything but nothing is going for you, hope begins with a laugh. (You are your own best joke. Very laughable.) Hope begins when you can laugh at yourself for thinking you are everything when God made you something else.

A sad, serious world needs a few fools . . . foolish people for Christ's sake. Fools sing when everyone else complains. They can worship God with a laugh while others debate his reality with dead seriousness. The fools for Christ hang loose with hope as the dead right find fault, find scapegoats. Fools can laugh. God has found them out, but yet they hope —and live.

What you do, how you feel, what you say, where you are is not the last chapter. You are not everything. Neither are you nothing. You can laugh at yourself for thinking you were the end of it all. God's played a joke on death. Jesus lives.

A dead serious world will not welcome fools, much less fools for Christ. Fools are free . . . free from being everything and free for being something else. The deadbeats can't stand such playfulness. You remind them of laughter—and they're afraid to laugh at themselves for they have never laughed at God's joke on death. When they think they are everything, death reminds them they are only something.

But the fool is something *else*. He laughs at himself, even when it hurts. He pokes fun at the obvious, at routine, at the old. He knows that's not all there is—everything. His laughing play may not open all doors,

but he believes not all doors are closed.

For God tells the story—a God who throws parties for angels when a sinner repents, a God whose foolishness is wiser than man's. God's fool can make light of what the dead serious have made heavy; the fool believes in the Resurrection—God's act of freeing the tight and making the heart light. God's spinning the story, saying all things are possible in spite of everything. God's something else too.

A laugh is hope. In laughing, fools are born. But the birth of fools is the sign of resurrection—for what was thought to be final is really the beginning. Fools for Christ have passed out of death into life. They're something else to those who are nothing at all—and together they laugh at believing one was everything and the other nothing. For each is something only in one another.

Dead seriousness is a dead end. It's an old, old story of Mr. Everything. But laughing hope is a new story—for fools only, for those who enjoy a surprise.

DEAD ENDS

When you are young, you want life to taste new, to move suddenly, to make sense, to groove. But it doesn't. It zigs and zags, jutting to the left and skidding to the right and bouncing flat. You call "heads" yet it always seems to end up "tails." You ask for a light, but get a burnt match. What is said and what is done come out in different shapes. Some say to you, "Cheer up!" but you know that if they ever smiled, their faces might crack. Inside you feel like jumping, but you sit still in your fear. You put on a happy face; still, it can't cover up your downbeat moods. Zig and zag and zoom.

When you are young, you yearn for fittings (ties that match your socks) . . . meetings (sockets that fit your light bulbs) . . . balance (answers to even your questions) . . . exchanges (lips pressed on lips) . . . companions (like thirst and coke). But life tips, ricochets, and vibrates. Little is smooth, even. You feel at odds. When you're polka-dot, others are plaid. Become a plaid and the world becomes stripes.

The contradictions, the differences, the ambiguities, the disagreements, the paradoxes, the discrepancies—

squeeze and twist and bend the eager beat of life.

Life is "Aagh!" It's nausea. "Aagh!" —a ripping sigh from tightly stretched feelings; a gasp leaking out of punctured hearts; a grunt of a beaten spirit; the hiss of hope running out of steam; a steady dripping of enthusiasm from a broken faucet. It's choking on melancholy.

It's "Aagh!" with parents. "Aagh!" for the heavy rules. "Aagh!" for the nagging "you should do this and you should do that." More "Aaghs!" for boring talk, hounding shouts, and crabby faces. It's "Aagh!" among the zig zags. No zip or zap.

Perhaps the sharpest "Aagh!" you stick into yourself. What you are and what you want to become feel miles apart. You wonder: Am I a "lemon," a misfit, a verse out of rhyme? Am I a switch that is off more than on? A ten chapter book with only one chapter? A movie with sound but no picture? You wonder, as knotty disgust tightens you inside: Who put the glue in my freedom? Is there a lot to live? After the dry days and dead ends?

It's like you're walking along a path. But suddenly walls stand before and around you. You change directions. Left. Then right. Zig. Zag. You stop. But you want to go. You hear voices saying to you—

"You can't move the walls. Can you climb it? Too high, huh? Well, stay put. You're going to look for a door? Okay, but. What? Did you find a door? Good. It's locked. You don't have a key. Wait your chance.

"Now where are you going? To see if there's another door. You won't listen. There is! What? It doesn't have a knob on it. Try prying it open with a knife. Hmm, that won't do it. Push your weight against it. Harder. Again. It still won't open. Use your knife again. No? It won't budge. Are you sure? Okay, okay, you're positive. Take a break. Give it a good kick!

"Where are you running? I can't hear you. Oh, you see another door. Why are you stopping? Someone slammed the door in your face. Oh, no! Scream! Holler! Shout! Tell him to open it. Why doesn't he open the door? He keeps saying that he doesn't want any. I bet he thinks you're a salesman. Tell him you're not. He refuses to open the door . . .

still saying he doesn't want any. Reason with him. Tell him you have an I.D. card and good references. No luck? Forget it. Curse him! Throw paint on the door. That'll show the fool.

"It's hopeless. What did you say? One more try. Okay. It's your life. What sign? There's a sign. What does it say? Exit. Don't go through it. You have to find an entrance door. I can't hear you. You're shouting too loud. You're making me mad.

"What are you doing now? You're going too far away. How will you find the path again? Why don't you listen to me? Stop shouting at me! What do you mean, you never asked for my opinion? It's your own fault. Don't blame me."

Dead ends. An exit instead of an entrance. No key, no knobs. Closed doors, slammed doors. "Stay put." "Curse—Kick." "Take a break." "Don't blame me."

Disgust. "Aagh!"

What's the use? So what? Who cares? Forget it!

But why? Can't polka dots go with plaids? Are doors only to be kicked? How about knocking? If there is a door marked "Out," maybe there's an "In"? Giving up? "Aagh"?

Disgust is the inability to choose new possibilities for yourself. It's a rut. Stuck. Bruised. Cheated. Bullied. Shut out. Abused. Bent.

But it's more than that. If life loses its color, you're the one who can color it. For disgust can be more than a mood. It may hang on and turn into a style of life. Perhaps a style of death? A habit of dying? After all, disgust is death pinching you—real hard and all over and again and again.

Besides, death is ambitious. It doesn't want to close only the back door, but the front door and all doors too. The strong desire of death is not reserved for after 30, the end, later. It wants your nows. For disgust is death compressed into the moment. "Aagh!" is the echo of its biting pinch.

Death's ambitiousness wants to drain your energies, to empty the cup of possibility, to scratch out your dreams, to eat away at your ripening expectations, to narrow what's up ahead by shrinking what's at hand.

When death in the disguise of disgust gets the most and best of you, your style of life tapers. Thin hopes. Small openings. Shy courage. You may settle into boredom, which is simply selling life short. Ho-humming your way through life, you are dull . . . worn smooth. You have no sharp point of view; you feel powerless; you think you don't count; you collapse your confidence; you judge yourself—you're nobody; you don't believe in yourself; you don't believe in much of anything. What's possible? Not much! Not even a hearty, defiant "Aagh!" Only a limp, "Oh, well."

Or, you can turn to self-pity. Poor me! I'm picked on! You become as disgusted with others as you are with yourself. For self-pity licks its wounds by accusing, damning others. Then you put icing on your complaints with exaggeration and overstatement.

Everything is the *worst;* nothing *ever* works; you *always* lose. What's possible? Very little! The "Aagh!" inside —too hot to handle—boils over into "Damn it all!"

Or, you can frantically clutch everything. "Now or never. At once. Presto. Right now!" It's all or nothing. You are ready to destroy anything— your own dreams, your own courage, your own judgment, your own neighbor. To smash all doors at any costs is the mad reaction of believing in death. Disgust is a tantrum death throws into your life—a wild fever of grabbing, demanding, seizing. What's possible? Nothing! A violent "Aagh!" —"The hell with everything."

Giving up, tantrums, curses, kicking, inflated accusations—then the haunting hush. And a strange whisper after the whirlwind, "Why not?"